The Trumpet Lily

Melania Trump - First Lady Of The United States

Richard Ilnicki

ISBN (Print Edition): 978-1-09832-575-6

ISBN (eBook Edition): 978-1-09832-576-3

MELANIA TRUMP
FIRST LADY OF THE UNITED STATES

THE TRUMPET LILY
POEMS BY RICHARD ILNICKI

This book is dedicated to Melania Trump

FLOTUS

"The only gift better than a book
is time enough to read it."

R.A. Ilnicki

"Your body follows your mind.
Where are you taking yours?"

R. A. Ilnicki

"You can make God be
whatever you want him to be,
but you can't make him be what he is not."

R. A. Ilnicki

"Every man I meet is in some way
my superior. In that I learn from him."

Ralph Waldo Emerson

"I never met a man I didn't like."

Will Rogers

Melania Table of Contents

1. "Mother-of-Pearl"   1
2. The Quintessential Poem   2
3. Melania, From a Distance   4
4. When She Plants Her Seeds   5
5. Melania Trump (The First Lady)   6
6. Her Trumpet Lilies   7
7. Melania Cuts Her Own Path   8
8. The Scent of Melania   9
9. Meet My Dream   10
10. The Last Flower Still Lives   11
11. Melania Speaks Out Against Bullying   12
12. Send in the Clowns   13
13. You Are The Center Of My Universe   14
14. How Do You Speak To An Angel?   15
15. Faithfully Look for Good News   16
16. Collateral Damage   17
17. Your Next Breath   18
18. Forgiveness   19
19. Watch Melania Spin   20
20. Yes, She Gets Angry   21
21. Today She Feels Like A Teardrop   22
22. Today I Feel Like a Confederate Statue   23
23. Our Astronomy   24
24. The View   25
25. Freedom of Speech   26
26. Canceled   27
27. Free at Last   28
28. When I Stand Before My God   30
29. Me Thinks Thou Doth Protest Too Much   31

30. The Pen Is Mightier Than The Sword   32

31. "Let Him Who Is Without Sin Cast The First Stone."   33

32. I Speak Five Languages   34

33. Social Distancing   35

34. Masks   36

35. Hate Is A Four-Letter Word   37

36. Season Your Speech With Love   38

37. Be Best, Be Kind, Judge Not   39

38. Don't Lock Me Down Alone   40

39. Pleiades Has An 8th Sister   41

40. We Are Not In Heaven Yet   42

Epilogue

41. Those Colorful White-hooded White Supremacists   44

42. James Brown's Posthumous Voice   46

43. White-Eyed Savages   47

44. Far Be It From Me   49

45. Blessed Beyond Measure   53

46. Love In The Age Of Psychiatry   54

47. Ethnic Cleansing: A War of Genes   57

48. "What Good Shall I Do This Day?"   59

"Mother-of-Pearl"

Melania

We are surrounded for now
by what seems to be
an invisible force.
We have been enclosed,
and it appears as if there is now way out.

Not only that, but.....
but as the pressure increases
we are further squeezed
into a space that keeps shrinking.
As the space inside the ball of fear shrinks
due to an unknown invader
the fear inside also increases
and panic replaces hope and reason. But..

But the good news is
we are being drawn closer and closer together.
Something good is emerging.
It is just as if we are oysters being clammed-up
by some outside force; the greater the pressure
the more positive the response.
It is this insidious irritant, a new disease,
a foreign substance,
that will bring the best out of us.

This foreign invader produces a defensive response
inside the oyster. With its defenses up
the oyster produces layer after layer of nacre,
also known as Mother-of-Pearl.
This protective reaction of the Mother-of-Pearl
brings forth the birth of the most beautiful pearls.

This is an opportunity for "America The Beautiful"
to "Come Together." Right now!

The Quintessential Poem

Melania Trump

Somewhere a poem resides hidden
beneath a coat of many colors,
rainbow's pot of gold on either end.
It is complete, lacks nothing
and contains every line ever written.
It lives beyond the sight and grasp of mortal man.

Perhaps it has been weaved silver-threaded
into the liquid air of kinetic energy,
a mythological bridegroom's love song.
Metaphysically, it has a mindset
capable of releasing miracles into the heart
of chosen believers.
Perhaps it can even bring to the famished heart
the same miracle rain that Elijah knew,
that mystical capability of transporting
more than one heavy laden cloud on its strong back.
Perhaps it can break the malevolent bars of bigoted prejudice
and set the innocent captive free.

This poem can live within the core of the sun
and not become thirsty, or it can hide behind
the fermented blue cheese moon of madness
and not be afraid of the dark.
Mythically, this muscular feminine being
is a conjugation of oxygenated blood and tempted flesh.

This poem lives and thrives
in a serene joyful place of perfect peace,
some uncharted geographical sanctuary.
It moves like an epiphany of celestial light
within its holy tabernacle
carrying one soft doe-eyed dove of peace

in its eternal bosom.

This poem is a symphony of No. 9 in D minor
indelibly written with the notes of unconditional love.
It is sung by the voice of forgiveness
and breaks the back of darkness.

Melania, From a Distance

Melania, from a distance
I have no problem speaking to her.
From a branch on the top of a tree, for example,
Or from a majestic mountain top,
Or some grand high tower.
Even from the shoulder of a cloud
would not be out of the question.

But, should I see her face to face,
I'm sure I would lose my nerve.
All that would roll off my tongue
would be similes and metaphors;
for example:

a red rose thorns bow down to,
a long drink of water for the thirsty,
a song of rhythmic bundled ribbons,
a flower seeding its own garden,
a cool breeze caught by surprise,
the subtle scent of homemade bread
cooling on the windowsill,
she's as lovely as the moonlight's comfort blanket
swaddling the earth,
or the sunrise gently waking sleeping flowers,
212 bones perfectly put together,
an erector set that moves with perfect posture and grace.

You know what I mean now, don't you?
I'd use language kinda like the above;
otherwise I wouldn't know what to say in her presence.
Frankly, I'd be tongue-tied.
So, for me, it's Melania from a distance,
a safe distance, lest I melt like ice cream in the sun.

When She Plants Her Seeds

Melania

When she plants her seeds
in The Rose Garden
she doesn't scatter them.
She plants each seed with purpose.

She walks with confidence
between the rows,
and each row welcomes her.

They are familiar with her nature,
and they know that winds to the contrary
no matter how arbitrarily administered
can uproot their future.

This compassionate gardener's sovereignty
fertilizes and waters them;
growth unspeakable is the joyful result.

When they crane their fragile necks
looking for her presence,
they receive strength and energy
as if it had just been provided by the sun.

They share blessed assurance and hope,
because they know she sees the future,
blooming exactly as it had been promised.

Melania Trump

(The First Lady)

As the First Lady
she moves like a precious flower
along the circle of the earth,
not carelessly, mind you.
She has a lot on her mind.

At other times you will find her
walking, seemingly, above the earth,
a type of angel in the disguise of a woman
seeking those whom she might encourage.

She wears her heart on her sleeve,
but she didn't place it there.
Her heart is exactly where it should be,
and it is obvious to those who know her.

You may not be sure where to find
The First Lady,
but when you do, you may find
that she often walks alone.
Based on who she is this might surprise you,
because she has company from
all around the world.

Furthermore, if you are found in her company
people will want to know who you are.
Who are you as to be so privileged to stand
in the company of The First Lady?

"King Charlemagne, it is my great privilege
to introduce you to Mrs. Melania Trump,
The First Lady Of The United States."

Her Trumpet Lilies

When we consider the lilies of the field
we must consider
that someone has been spinning them,
some seamstress in the disguise of a gardener.

Do you see her yarn?
Do you see her spinning wheel?
Watch her in the garden from your window.
See how seamlessly she threads the flowers;
watch closely as they emerge
as garments fit for a queen.

The yellow, the plum, the pink, the apricot,
and the glistening white to bright gold,
but don't forget the exceptionally beautiful
maroon petals on the outside of the Trumpet.

These Trumpet lilies have a heavy sweet fragrance.
They add distinction and elegance to the environment,
and they seem to invite you into their presence.

These magnificent garments of perennials
she has diligently been spinning,
are those that she will be wearing
to the next inaugural ball.

Melania Cuts Her Own Path

Come, let us walk together
through the beautiful garden of this life.
Let us take a straight path, an unrehearsed path,
filled with blooming mysteries.
However, we must be mindful
that if we continue to walk a straight path
we will surely miss spontaneous moments
found on the left and the right paths.

But we can't follow all paths
at the same time.
We must make choices,
but neither should we follow paths
others may have mapped out for us.

Ours is not necessarily to follow
paths others have taken
even after their glad return
filled with glowing reports.

Keen listening should be accorded them,
but a loving admonition delivered kindly
should just as kindly be received
if we have decided to cut our own path.

The Scent of Melania

(When Donald Saw Melania For the First Time)

I had been blinded
By past decisions made impetuously.
I'd been known to act spontaneously based on impulse.
So, perhaps I deserved to be
Grinding blinded like Samson
In a dungeon of despair surrounded by my enemies.

But, deep down inside
Where my broken heart resided
I wanted to see.
I wanted to see God's majestic hand
In the wonderful world around me,
Especially the unspeakable
Beautiful array of glorious flowers gracing the land,
Lilies in the valley, roses on the bush, lilacs in springtime,
And do not forget the Buttercups dusting up the landscape.

My smell was intact, thank God,
Because the first time
I got close enough to smell you,
He opened my eyes.

Meet My Dream

In the field of dreams
no matter how well populated
life would be meaningless
without dreamers.

These searchers,
who, hopefully become dream catchers,
come from all around the world.
They may not be seeking
the same dream,
but they have one thing in common.
They are looking for something
or someone special
they haven't met yet.

To some, maybe most,
there expectations are unrealistic.
But,
that is why they have been labeled
dreamers.
So go ahead, "Hitch your wagon to a star."

The Last Flower Still Lives

The last time he looked out of his window

the first flower was still standing.
The same thing happened the first time
he looked out of his window.
She was still standing
while bending the sun in her direction.
"This must be no ordinary flower," he thought.

Of course, he was tempted
to pick it,
but then it might die,
and he would be responsible
for 2nd degree manslaughter.
So, he thought better of it.

He believed
that as long as he was able
to look out of his window
the flower would remain.

"Perhaps someday it might be picked
by an innocent bystander
whose ignorance may be attributed to
a failing romance," he thought.

So, what do you think he did?
He picked it.

Melania Speaks Out Against Bullying

Bullies come in different shapes and sizes.
Neither is there any differentiation
according to sex, sexual orientation
or color.
Bullies are simply predators
who lack a conscience,
and they always seem to be looking
for someone to prey on,
usually someone who cannot fight back.

They are similar to a well-known virus
that is looking for a host.
The difference, however, is
they abuse others in the open
and take pride in doing so.

Bullies hate indiscriminately,
except in some cases,
such as in a case very close to me.
In this instance they have attached themselves
to the spouse
in an attempt to vindicate their hatred.

Beware, my fellow Americans,
your acrimonious vitriol
may someday boomerang,
and you may be the victim.

Send in the Clowns

They said, they wouldn't dress you.
They should have said,
we wouldn't know where to begin;
we're just a bunch of clowns.

Who are these arrogant designers?
They wouldn't recognize "Good taste"
if it came down an escalator
on the arm of the future president.

If they know what is good for them,
they should look in the mirror.
If their peach fuzz is showing
They should put Bozo in the tub with Little Ducky.
They should then take a mannequin to bed,
but only after they've had a cold shower.

You Are The Center Of My Universe

Nothing can ever be the same.
All things have changed for the better
Since I found you
Reclining Hair-blown against the wind.
Your discriminating taste in body languages
Shatters inferior mirror images,

> And the aura of your soul
> Has caused a paradigm shift in my heart.
> To me you are a revelation
> Like that which struck with incalculable force
> Copernicus between the eyes.
> Your surefooted steps climb my mountain
> Like biblical hinds' feet on high places.

You have rounded out the flat earth
Of people with small minds
Who fall with regularity
Like blind conscripted lemmings
Off the forbidden edge into the jaws of oblivion.

Your love has freed me
and protected me from sorrowful cynical people,
Men and women whose proud puffed-up chests
Have been loaded down with medals.

Ambitious, unkind, untrue, are those
Who would decry to the death

> Unconditional love's existence,
> Those who would arrogantly deny
> The purity of self- sacrifice
> And refuse to board a wooden ship
> Headed for the New World.

Richard Ilnicki

How Do You Speak To An Angel?

(Melania Speak)

How do you speak to an angel?
First things first,
you'd need to get close enough to her,
but how close could you get close enough
without being consumed
by the flame of her smile?

How could you get close enough
to get her attention?
Consider the crowds
of kings and queens and dignitaries surrounding her.
Furthermore,
What language would you presume to speak
in her presence?

Perhaps you wouldn't be able to speak at all.
Maybe you would stutter unintelligibly,
like a dumbstruck, tongue-tied fool,
or perhaps
you would be wise enough to speak to her
with the mysterious sound of eternity.

Yes, speak to an angel
from your heart
with roses on your lips
and stars on your tongue,
and surely, you will be heard.

Faithfully Look for Good News

When least expected He casts His shadow
Across my reclining flesh.
He knows my frame is but dust
And that I am an earthworm
Crawling through the mud of night.
He has a way of locating me
When I go missing; He is a sovereign omnipresent Father.
He knows just where to find His wayward child,

Whether on a familiar doorstep, in the alley
Or just standing leisurely on the corner.
He doesn't need to send a private eye.
He just sends Himself
In the convicting garment of The Holy Spirit.

Far too often He finds me
In a state of spiritual lethargy
Caught in a state of wearisome well-doing
But not doing well as The First Lady.

Here He finds
That I have become a woman undone,
But His shadow has power enough to raise the dead
And the living.

Without my permission His shadow
Scans my muddled mind and heavy heart,
                    And revives me!!!
He comes to me today
With an irresistible call; a heavenly exhortation
Of regeneration which brings me to my feet,

And He leads me in The Way
Which has been sovereignly spread before me
With the breadcrumbs of The Good News.

Richard Ilnicki

Collateral Damage

The battle began in the trenches
of the mouth,
the cylindrical cave of fire-breathing gushers
and bifurcated tongues.
The sensitive inviting taste buds
had been bathed in acid
rain from the heart's regurgitations.
The blood bath would come later
When her back was turned.

These innocent buds were unable to distinguish flavors,
and the throat was raw due to the malicious intentions
of a mustard gas eating poet.
No friend to cowards,
Poisonous metaphors filled his salivary glands
like ripe fruit hanging just within reach
of foreign fingers.

His untamed tongue was ready
to lick the floor with abandoned parts of speech;
parts begging for an opportunity
to join the fray on the front lines
right along with the other washed brains.

Your Next Breath

Your next breath is your next miracle.
Go ahead and take one and become conscious
Of the unconscious.
Play the voluntary lord over the involuntary
Then please be kind enough
To provide us with an understanding
Of the respiratory system,
Its faithfulness in the face of things unseen.

Explain the exchange of gases
Between an organism and the medium
Within which it lives,

Pharynx larynx epiglottis
And the mysterious exchange
Of oxygen and carbon dioxide in the lungs
And the necessary perfusion
Of the pulmonary tissues with adequate blood,
The pulmonary alveolus magic carpet ride!

Charismatic pedantic educator,
Explain how the medulla oblongata of the brain stem
Regulates the movements of respiration.
In conclusion
Explain your next miracle
And the biological synergy of creation.

Forgiveness

There exists a peculiar fragrance
In forgiveness.
It defies the empirical finite, those smells
Of sacrificial decomposing flesh, those subservient little lambs
Without spot or blemish and big innocent eyes.
Tied tightly to the altar of sacrifice,
Their slit throats above the fire drip.

Forgiveness brings to its knees and embarrasses
Even the kindest gesture,
The bravest action,
The purest motive,
The most faithful behavior; it shames
The sweetest flower's subtle invitation.

Forgiveness pollinates absolution in the garden
And sets the proud gardener free.

This peculiar fragrance breaks on purpose
The sun-dried leather skin of lust
Disguised as love,
                    Some impostor being
                    The final evisceration of the soul.

Forgiveness takes delight and watches
The liquid Balm of Gilead bathe the root of bitterness,
Seeds of anger manifesting hatred
Into absolute submission.

Knees down,
On the skin of knees begging
There exists
A peculiar fragrance in forgiveness;
It is the aroma of God,
The odor of His sacrifice.

Watch Melania Spin

Now
in this empty moment
surrounded by nothing
I want to get into the luggage.
My circumstances make me want to hide.

I want to become a part
of the baggage.
In this fashion I can hide
among the garments
and not be judged.

Maybe I can become
a piece of expensive silk,
a fashionable tie for the president
or a gorgeous gown for myself.

Or better yet,
become the worm
that spins the silk
seemingly out of nothing.

Yes, She Gets Angry

Equal opportunities abounded
    And the land was soon flooded
        With would be entrepreneurs
            Carrying picks and shovels.
Most of them came from black town
Where they had learned to work
With their backs
Lifting the sun out of the earth,
Some stubborn orb which became
Hotter
      More dangerous.
        And more recalcitrant
          The closer you got,

But these men had brought with them
A well-kept secret.
They had learned
That you could coax the sun out
By sending the moon down
To where the sun don't shine.

Today She Feels Like A Teardrop

Today I feel like a teardrop
That has fallen into the arms
Of the opposition.
Before I began to cry,
I was being kept alive in secret
Where I spent all my time
In the company of friends.
We played together,
And when we got dirty
We bathed together
In the innocent lavender pool of Aphrodite.

Exhausted by anticipation
We remained tears in waiting.
We were innocent children born of our Father.
We had been primed by the oil of gladness
And promised that some day
We would be tears shed at the birth of a child
Or at a royal wedding.

But instead we have fallen hard
Into the arms of vengeance
And have sorrowfully landed
In the valley of dry eyes.

Today I Feel Like a Confederate Statue

Today I feel like a confederate statue
about to be pulled down
by an angry mob.
They don't like the way I look,
the way I dress,
the way I walk,
where I am from,
my historical roots,
my ancestry,
and, more importantly,
to whom I am married.

Our Astronomy

Have you ever felt astronomical?
I have.
I love to go into the Rose Garden,
unaccompanied.
I look up into the endless sky
with the wonderment of a child.
Sometimes I take Baron with me.
We can't see the other plants, comets or galaxies,
but we can see the stars.
They appear so far away, and they are.
When we want to bring the stars closer
we look into each other's eyes.

Richard Ilnicki

The View

The View
has a particularly peculiar view of me.
Their view is based
not so much on me. Their view
is based on who I am married to.
They have not had me on lately,
and they probably won't,
lest they recognize me as being human.
Furthermore, I am a woman just like them.
Maybe not quite like them
or even other women; we're all different in some regard.

They all probably have good taste,
but they find me hard to swallow.
Perhaps they are afraid
they won't know how to speak to me.
After all I only speak five different languages;
I might be hard to understand;
they prefer to understand me
the way they see me.

I surmise, perhaps improperly
and unfortunately for me,
as the First Lady,
that if I were black
or married to a black man,
they might consider having me on
as a Guest. Not necessarily, however,
because their intolerance and uncompromising
view of me
Trumps their compassion and love
for those they disagree with.
Black Live Matter, but so do the lives
Of those you may disagree with.

Freedom of Speech

They told me
in no uncertain terms
that they believe in
freedom of speech.

And, they do,
until you open your mouth
and disagree with them.

I also found
they have a common and effective way
of shutting you down
by shouting you down.

"Let Freedom Ring!"

Canceled

We had a pretty popular show.
Our viewer-ship was up,
and our ratings topped the charts.
Our sponsors loved us,
but we were summarily canceled.

They said my great, great, grandfather
had used black-face
when he played Othello
at the Globe Theater in London.
I think it was around 1599
or shortly thereafter.

Free at Last

(Parental Bullying)

This was his father's workshop.
His metaphorical square circle,
An arena and/or coliseum; his cellar
Where he lived out his gladiatorial fantasies.
Here, he frequently drew blood
From the innocent noses of his sons.
Those soft 16 oz. Gloves were for sissies.

Besides tools, guns and knives
He had a black & white TV
And a clock radio on the shelf above the table saw.
Dad was 'all man.' and believed that
"Winners never quit, and quitters never win."
He could probably swallow swords,
Eat fire on a stick, Force Paul Bunyan
To submit to a Figure Four Grapevine,
Or KO Rocky Marciano with a right cross.

But on this day
A real live dragon slayer showed-up,
A sight and match for which dad was not prepared.

The young man had come
To strategically position himself in a chair,
A throne fashioned from cold-rolled steel.
The psychologically fire-forged legs
Had been buried deep inside cast-iron ingots,
Leftover weapons from the war.
He'd practiced securing the shotgun in a vice
With the trigger of the weapon
Within reach of his big toe.
When the time was right
He would load his father's shotgun,

Push the trigger with his toe
And blow his brains out.

There would be no
Second-guessing his bravery, this time!
No kidney punches, no rabbit punches,
And no low blows, just solid combinations,
Conjunctions, consonants, adverbs and adjectives
In the guise of similes and metaphors
Meant to emasculate his opponent.

He pushed the trigger on a Sunday
When his father was working overtime.
The other family members were in church
Saying prayers, lighting candles and taking
A much-needed communal break from sin
And their conflicted Catholic consciences.

The celebratory, tragic, and cowardice,
By some standards, act proved quite successful.
The young man's brains
Were splattered all over the garage floor and walls.
Most of his subconscious graced the canvas
Of the boxing ring with flowers.

In a neutral corner, the coroner acting as a referee,
Found a preponderance of his left hippocampus
Along with bloody, ganglionated spinal memories,
Hauntings that had voided the merging of hemispheres,
The prohibition to make peace with his past.

When I Stand Before My God

Hebrews 4:13

When I stand before my God
I want to be clothed with thick coverings.
I want layer upon layer of clothes
To hide the secret iniquities within,
Those sins known only to myself.
I want to swaddle my shame like a mummy
With the perfumed threads of Egypt.
I want to be covered head to toe,
Then hidden in the catacombs
                    Until He calls me by name.
Even then,
When I hear His voice
I want to be able to play deaf,
Though I know when He calls, He calls
With a voice which is irresistible.
Yet I also know
Despite my reluctance and fear of exposure,
The obvious embarrassment and humiliation
Of my disobedience,
I will stand before Him without excuse,
And I will watch my clothes of hypocrisy
Fall off in sloughed, soiled, layered heaps.

When I stand before my God
                    I will be naked,

Though clean enough, pure enough
And unashamed enough
To wear the white robe of righteousness
His Son will have provided.

Me Thinks Thou Doth Protest Too Much

Me thinks thou doth protest too much,
not enough, or wrongly so.
Let him who hath no soundness in his soul,
no sound of protestation in his cells,
keep silent,
lest he speak up at the wrong time
and therewith be defiled.

Better not to have spoken at all
than to speak up
with the sound of ignorance.

Doth thou dare protest this protest
at a time of cellular differentiation
based on cellular division?
I pray not.

We must not only speak up
when we have first been spoken to.
We must speak up
when we have something important to say,
something that will bring a change for the better.

My exhortation, though, would be
to those who protest,
to speak peaceably with the roar of reason
from a throat unthrottled and free.

"La plume est plus forte que l'epee"

The Pen Is Mightier Than The Sword

Language doesn't need to be foul
in order to be foul.
It just needs to be potentially harmful
and punitive on some level.
The foulest language I've heard
is language directed at someone
to humiliate, demean or belittle them.

Language, whether spoken or written,
can essentially serve one of two ends:
it can encourage, or it can discourage.
You can build someone up
or you can tear them down.

Mark Twain said,
"I can live two months on a good compliment."
Napoleon said,
"Four hostile newspapers are more to be feared than
1,000 bayonets."

Silence is not necessarily golden, but it can be
if the tongue is about to become a flaming fire.

"See how great a forest a little fire kindles!
And the tongue is a fire, a world of iniquity.
The tongue is so set among our members
that it defiles the whole body and sets on fire the course of nature,
and it is set on fire by hell......but no man can tame the tongue.
It is an unruly evil, full of deadly poison.
With it we bless God, and with it we curse men
who have been made in the similitude of God." James 3:5-9

As for me, "Set a guard, O Lord, over my mouth;
keep watch over the door of my lips." Psalms 141:3-4

"Let Him Who Is Without Sin Cast The First Stone."

It's not that they all dislike me
because I'm The First Lady.
Some people do like me.
The problem is not
that everyone should like me.
Nobody is liked by everyone,
unless you are Mr. Rogers.

My problem is they are judging me
on my past, my present,
and probably my future.

I would be the first one to admit
that I am a sinner; maybe not
the chief of sinners,
but I'm certainly bad enough
and probably could be even worse.

It's just that they have surrounded me,
and I can't turn my back to them.
If I could run to the "Wailing Wall"
I would, but as it is,

the stones they will be throwing
will be coming from all directions,
and I have nowhere to hide.

I Speak Five Languages

I speak five languages.
So what!
Sure, it may be a sign of my gift
of language comprehension,
and the capacity to speak to people
in their own language.
It might even make me seem to be
of above average intelligence.
So what!

According to author Gary Chapman
there are "Five Love Languages."
These are the five languages
I would like to speak fluently with grace:

1. Words of Affirmation
2. Gifts
3. Acts of Service
4. Quality Time
5. Physical Touch

I have found these to be universal languages
that anyone can speak.
I'm hard at work daily
learning how to be a better speaker
of these wonderful languages. The good news
about these languages is:

"I am my own teacher, and my fluency
depends solely on me. At the end of each day
I have the opportunity to grade myself."

Social Distancing

Based on the current pandemic
social distancing
has become the new normal.

It is a good policy;
it makes sense
and it works.
Staying six feet apart
seems to be effective.

In my presence
this new policy
is easy to keep,
because a lot of people
wouldn't touch me
with a 10 foot pole.

Masks

Wearing masks
to protect others
is a good policy.
This policy is not new to me.
In fact,
Washington D.C.
is the only place
where masks are common.

In fact,
This may be the only place
in our country
where masks have always been
commonly worn.

So much for transparency.

Hate Is A Four-Letter Word

I've met people who hate me.
People I have not met also hate me.
People who know nothing about me hate me.
People who do know certain things about me hate me.
If it were possible,
people who are indifferent would also hate me.
Some people hate indiscriminately
and are intolerable of others' opinions.

I think
if people would take the time
to get to know me better,
they wouldn't hate me.
They may not love me, but
they wouldn't hate me.

There are people I disagree with;
I think and believe differently than they do,
but I don't hate them,
and I hope and pray
that I never will hate them.

Hate is a four-letter word in any language.
It may be spelled differently,
but, by definition, it means the same thing.
Hate is a four-letter word.

Season Your Speech With Love

I've always admired good speakers.
Obviously, I never heard Demosthenes speak,
neither have I heard William Jennings Bryan speak,
but I have heard Martin Luther King, Jr. speak.
His command of the audience's attention
was partly based
on his command of the English language.
Mahatma Gandhi was also a great speaker;
he could speak for hours without notes.

Besides these two men's speaking ability,
something else bound them inextricably together.
That common element was love.
Love for the common man, the downtrodden,
the misbegotten, the underdog, the outcasts,
the untouchables, the forgotten men and women.

There have also been
numerous other great orators,
some more captivating than others.
Hitler and Goebbels, for example, were great orators.
Which just goes to show you
that some speakers are motivated by hate,
a sense of superiority, a malignant narcissism,
and sad to say,
these have had audiences with willing ears.

"Though I speak with the tongues of men and of angels
and have not love, I have become sounding brass
or a clanging cymbal." 1st Co. 13:1

Be Best, Be Kind, Judge Not

I've been around a lot of judges.
Judges are necessary,
and most judges are fair.
They do their best
to uphold the law.
They usually get it right,
but sometimes they don't.
It seems to me
that when they don't,
outside influences distort their judgment.
It's usually money, power or politics.

Of course, the law is quite important,
and the Constitution needs to be upheld.
My position is to obey the law, but,

but there is another law that concerns me.
It's the law governed by love,
supported by kindness, compassion,
and the exhortation to not judge another.
To not judge another
because they are different than you,
or because they don't agree with you,
your particular point of view on politics, religion,
economics, immigration, education,
or any other matter of importance.

"Judge not, that you be not judged. For with
what judgment you judge, you will be judged,
and with what measure you use, it will be
measured back to you." Matthew 7:1-2.

Don't Lock Me Down Alone

When I am alone,
quarantined off limits and forbidden
to communicate, I find comfort
in my family, friends and books.
I don't like to be cooped up and locked down
with nothing but my thoughts.
I don't like this lonely corner of my mind.
I find an exponential degree of isolation squeezes me
out into the open where I can share
what is on my mind.

An obstreperous vacuous emptiness
surrounds me if I am locked down for too long.
My website loses its sturdy legs
and no spider weaving intrigue remains
to wrap and prepare me for the existential bite.

In this undeclared time zone
I can hear a pin drop in China,
and, furthermore, I can hear the grass growing
and a squirrel's heart beating.

All that is left for me to embrace
in this semi-private room
I am sharing with death
is the rhythmic beating of a guilty heart,
a silent sound begging me to confess
that I desire to be sealed
beneath the floorboards with the one I love.

Richard Ilnicki

Pleiades Has An 8th Sister

Say to the sky, "Who is your mother?"
Who had the nerve to give you such liberty?"
Such presumption is repulsive
And borders on insanity.
Who could have been so naïve
As to sincerely believe
You wouldn't abuse it?

Why, just look at you!
Look at how much space
You have occupied
At the expense of other visionaries.
Don't you have at least a modicum of humility?
Didn't your mother teach you
To share with others,
Especially those less fortunate than yourself,
And, "No!"
I don't mean the sun, the moon,
The stars or some lesser known planets.

What I mean is, "What about her?"
Why can't she bathe in The Milky Way
And become the astronomical focus
Of professional stargazers?
Why can't she be on the chart of the sky
And play a meaningful part in someone's horoscope?

Why not grant Melania the privilege
Of hitching her wagon to a star? If not,
Then why not let her nonchalantly dangle
From some invisible string
And be recognized as celestial?

We Are Not In Heaven Yet

It is obvious
to all who have been informed,
and even to those
who have not been informed,
that we are not in Heaven, yet.

Why not?

Because, all things being equal
we are all equal in Heaven.
"There is neither Jew nor gentile,
male nor female,
slave nor free."
Furthermore, there is no strife, no hatred,
no division, no anger, no malice,
no slander, no libel, no blasphemy;
neither is there any other behavior
that does not glorify the God
who created us to love one another.

It must be obvious, then,
that there will never be a 'Heaven on earth.'

But,
How close can we get?

I guess it all depends
on whether or not we believe
that all lives matter.

Epilogue

An epilogue is the concluding section that rounds out the design of a literary work; the seven following poems are not necessarily that, but the sentiment is that "All men are created equal," or should have been, or should be, but have not been, and still aren't, except in the eyes of God.

We live in a great country with a multitude of shortcomings, but our country will always be a 'work in progress.' I have shortcomings, and I am a 'work in progress.' Everyday I have opportunities to manifest the Fruit of The Spirit, beginning with love followed by joy, peace, long-suffering, kindness, goodness, faithfulness, gentleness, self-control, and, I would like to add meekness.

"Never look down on anybody unless you are helping them up."
"Humility is not thinking less of yourself; it is thinking of yourself less."
"Humility, that low, sweet root, from which all heavenly virtues shoot."
"Humility is the proper estimate of oneself."
"It's amazing what you can accomplish if you do not care who gets the credit."
"It is unwise to be too sure of one's own wisdom. It is healthy
to be reminded that the strongest might weaken, and the wisest might err."

Muhammad said, "The best of people is the one who humbles himself the more his rank increases."

I hope the reader recognizes my intention to communicate honestly with integrity, and that my desire is to improve upon what God had stated. Obviously, I have a way to go.

"A house divided against itself cannot stand." Abraham Lincoln
June 16, 1858.

Those Colorful White-hooded White Supremacists

For Rosa and Martin

The sycophant black inhabitants of graves
Stacked in layers of sloughed flesh
Peeled themselves free from the blood
Of obsequious centuries.
The plasma of their voices had been rudely coagulated.
They'd been closed by fear and bark collars
Designed to 'dumb them down'
But Now!
But now they were shouting 'at the top'
Of ten thousand voices
Times ten thousand voices:
"Free at last!
Free at last!
Good God Almighty, We're Free at last!"

They came dancing.
They came clapping.
They came singing
They came jumping out of the stereotypical wood pile
> out from beneath the hot Alabama Sun,
> down from the swinging noose of narcissism,
> down from the auction block like cattle,
> up from the valley of blood-stained cotton,
> up from the prejudice of blighted pigments,
> down from up, and up from down, they came
> Up From Slavery!

Yes, they had finally been resuscitated and emancipated
From the blight of black ball and chain
By the timely death of another. Good God All Mighty,
Free at last! They continued to pinch themselves and shout
Free at last! Good God All Mighty, we're free at last!

Joyfully they slid beneath the ivory lid
To share the air space inside his majestic coffin.
They moved like invading bad memories
Once covered by humiliated skin, contused bones,
Poor self-images and lower than the lowest self-esteem.

The dictator was dead, and he was now their equal.
They removed him from his bed of flowering ease,
Stripped him naked in front of his children,
Hosed him down with a fire hose
Then luxuriously bathed him in a tub of burning crosses.
Next, his emaciated sin-soaked soul, eviscerated of blood,
Was hung from a tree, but he wasn't left to die.
They left him swinging low sweet chariot
Then cut him down after he'd turned dark blue.

                    After a short revival they tarred and feathered him
And wrapped him like a mummy
In second-hand grave clothes…stained by black-eyed peas,
                    Collard greens, the sparse marrow of neck bones,
                            And the small intestines of pigs.

With the drums still beating
And the smell of victory in the air
Black ghosts dressed in white shadows exited the coffin
In a ceremonial display of rhythm and blues.

Finally! In a celebratory piece de resistance
They dragged him down a dank dark street
In a God forsaken rat infested ghetto.
They then made him ride alone
For an eternity
In the back of a yellow bus in Selma, Alabama
Being chased by German Shepherds.

James Brown's Posthumous Voice

(Say It Loud)

Sometimes change comes
as if by accident, some unexpected event,
a paradigm shift that moves the quaking earth beneath its feet,
some fault, some default, some seismic tectonic shift.
The shift is sudden, or so it seems,
anticipated by no one
and most especially not by evolutionary men,
fossils who have grown feathers
and have lived as oblivious ostriches.

These men's bigoted big heads have been buried
in the sand of denial for centuries.
These Neanderthals, living in the caves of the past,
had never been emancipated
from the chains of hate that bound them.
They are the offspring of hieroglyphs
and had never recognized that
the handwriting on the wall spelled E Q U A L I T Y.

When these 'so-called' men pull their hooded heads
out of the sand and look around
they shall be witnesses against themselves,
and willingly or not, on that guilty day,
they will confess and admit that, indeed!

"Papa's Got a Brand-New Bag"

and, furthermore, that...........................
that old mournful "Old Black Joe" song
will be a joyful refrain of the unshackled singing:

"I'm Black and I'm Proud!"
"I'm Black and I'm Proud!"
"I'm Black and I'm Proud!"

White-Eyed Savages

A heart pounding horse cavalry of biblical legions
Was riding heady/high-minded roughshod,
To the cry of malignant narcissism unleashed.
These West Point White Anglo Saxon Protestants
Were galloping orderly and confidently
Across the plains of Indian sovereignty.
These gentlemanly quarterlies were blazing
A trail of tears
Filling their boots with bloody laughter.

The guttural brass bugle charge
Had been loudly sounded while busting
The friendly eardrums of The Spirit in the Sky.
The innocent landscape filled with hope
Was being ruptured like an infected useless spleen,
A land composed of vestigial organs
Disguised as humans.
This fecund virgin land was about to be emptied
Of its passion and promise by an army of liars.

These genetically superior pure genes
Came violently slicing
          and splicing
            and separating
Red Cloud from Cochise, Cochise from Sitting Bull,
Sitting Bull from Powhatan, Powhatan from Geronimo,
Geronimo from Crazy Horse, etc.
Until all red men had been separated
From the God of wind, rain, and snow,
And the sun and the moon and the stars
And the corn and the…………………..

Shod with sickle and scythe,
Guns, cannons and holy scriptures

These well-groomed, sophisticated men came raping

Young corn still on the husk.
Their saddled compliant horseflesh
Was being whipped into a rabid frenzy
By Blue Coats pursuing Buffalo Men riding bareback.
They were chasing faithful Braves,
Brave men who possessed bows and arrows for hunting
To feed their squaws and shiny red-skinned children.

This army of brass had been schooled on
Square roots and the classics; they were
Educated civil men of high degree,
But they had halitosis; blood was on their breath,
And the sweat on their skin oozed bigotry.
These White Eyes were malignant narcissistic savages at heart
And represented the blind
Leading the blind into a ditch of their own making.
These soldiers were refined Ivy-leaguers,
And they knew exactly which fork to use and when.
They always washed their dirty hands before meals,
Said Grace,
                    And they wouldn't dare think
Of eating a buffalo liver with bare hands.
Furthermore, the medals gracing their puffed-up chests
Were solid refined gold proof
That they considered collecting scalps
To be well below their dignity.

"The Indians must go. They couldn't be exterminated whole-
sale because of world opinion, but they could be uprooted and
packed off to some remote corner of the country where they
wouldn't be in the way."

Andrew Jackson had pledged himself to the policy of
Indian Removal.
Any Indian who remained on his ancestral lands affirming his
Indian identity would be a criminal.

Far Be It From Me

Far be it from me
to tell you what it is like to live
in a "Death camp."
I humbly and candidly submit
that I have no idea what it is like.
I've never smelled
the blood bathed bodies
bobbing like dead catfish in a barrel,
or smelled seared human flesh
cooking or spinning on a spit.
I've never smelled human ashes,
the cremated remains, blanketing
the campground like snow.
I've never smelled mounds of stacked, decaying,
putrefying human research paper,
rat fodder.
I've never smelled fear, doubt, worry, anxiety,
uncertainty, bitterness, and hatred to the degree
that they became anthropomorphic,
inhabited human flesh and buried faith alive.

I've never smelled the stench of eviscerated souls
devoid of hope then expelled as foul from the bowels.
I wasn't there when the screams
of cadaver anatomy being performed
on living humans filled the four corners
of the camp with the blood of busted eardrums.
I've never heard the screams
of throats being strangled by nightmares
nor the specter of laughing apparitions
dancing on the wall like imaginary assassins.
I've never heard the cry of raped wombs
nor the squeal of sodomized infants.

I've never heard the sound of prayers

being poisoned by gas
then left unspoken in collapsed black lungs.
I've never heard the sound of a locomotive's
iron horse wheels
delivering screeching boxcars packed with death.
I've never heard the mortified wail of conjoined twins
being cleaved into two by a "Doctor of Death"
for experiment's sake and a brighter future.

I've never seen men and women
being paraded naked in files of humiliation
with no covering to hide their shame.
I've never seen real live zombies
dressed in pinstripes meandering
around in hallucinogenic stupors.
I've never seen mounds of naked corpses
being bulldozed into an open grave
like hopelessly ill cattle suffering
from "mad cow disease"
as a malignant threat to humans.
I've never seen a dropped victim
fully extend the rope
while the hangman's knot causes
fracture dislocation of the upper cervical spine
and transection of the spinal cord.

I've not seen these men, women and children
swinging in the wind like pinatas
emptied of their colorfully candied intestines.
I've not seen exhausted men
afraid to fall asleep, victims of hypnophobia,
who sleep with one eye open.
I've never seen men, women and children
packed together like sardines
bathed in a solution of mustard gas.

I've never seen human beings

Richard Ilnicki

numbered and branded like cattle
then whimsically slain by laughing butchers.

I've never seen seraphim, cherubim and guardian angels,
trapped in nets like frightened fish
then plucked of every holy feather
by devils in hobnailed combat boots.
No, I've never seen the holy face of God
distorted and disfigured melting in the flames
like some plastic superstitious icon,
hope torn from the dashboard
by third degree despairing hands baking in an oven.
I've never seen men clinging an electrified barbed wire fence
begging for the voltage.

I've never had my jaws pried open
while my teeth were yanked from my mouth
without an ounce of Novocain.
I've never tasted the blood of my brother
or held his crushed skull in my hands.
I've never cuddled with a corpse to keep warm.
I've never lusted after a pair of shoes
on a dead man.

No, I've never had my mind strapped
to the Bed of Procrustes and then stretched
to the point that I would abandon my family
or deny my God.
I've never had my wife, the love of my life,
or my children, my God-given full quiver,
torn violently from my arms
and suffer, thereby, the unspeakable
pain of terminal separation.
Would I ever see them again in this life?
In this hell? If I did,
would I want to gaze upon their emaciated
skeletal bodies broken by hopelessness?

Or, would I prefer to remember them
as they once were, flowers dancing
into and out of my strong and tender arms?
I've never walked beneath the Sword of Damocles
afraid to make one false move
lest I get shot between the eyes
or through the heart from the tower.

No, I have not suffered from lycanthropy,
the plague of Nebuchadnezzar, gone mad
and been forced to eat grass like an ox
as some of these men have.
I've not had to survive the slings and arrows
of outrageous fortune in the guise of malignant narcissism.
No, I have not been forced to behave like an animal
from a lower phylum
while keeping company with amoebas and paramecium.

I've never been treated like a man
whose behavior is lower than sin.
No, I have not seen, smelled, heard, touched
nor tasted death as have these men
women and children,
but I can do my best to see to it that we
ought to do unto others
as we would have others do unto us.

We ought to love our neighbors as ourselves.
This, I can do, and far be it from me
to do otherwise,
because in the sight of God all lives matter.

Blessed Beyond Measure

If I were to measure my blessings
I would clearly see
that I have been blessed beyond measure.
How is it then
that sometimes you will find me complaining?
I have nothing to complain about,
at least nothing
that is monumental in nature.
I'm embarrassed when I complain,
and I should be.

Besides having been
"Fearfully and wonderfully made
and skillfully wrought in the lowest parts of the earth,"
I am an immigrant
who has become the First Lady Of The United States.
I have learned that this is not necessarily
the most enviable position a woman can hold,
but I am doing my best. I am doing my best
based on where I am, who I am,
and those with whom I keep company

I am showered with blessings every day.
In fact, I am completely drenched
even when it is not raining.

Be your best and do your best
with what you have been given right where you are,
and remember,
"Being the best is not as important as doing your best."

Love In The Age Of Psychiatry

When they put my wife summarily
into the psychiatric ward for her own good
and for the good of others,
they collapsed my suffering ventricles,
prolapsed my mitral valve
and rudely broke my already infarcted heart.

This emotional implosion scattered the shattered pieces
and other impossible to identify or gather fragments
like buckshot fired from an unfamiliar shotgun.
They might as well have left me tongue-tied
and abandoned on a doorstep in some foreign country.

This rude though necessary incarceration
sliced my rudely ruptured insides like a cleaver
in the hands of an Old World butcher.
The pain tore at my stubborn visceral organs like incisors
in love with the raw meat of uncontrolled emotions.
Intelligent explosive devices designed to annihilate personality
ripped into my hippocampus
and began to divide my exposed mind even further.

My fall had not been fatal, but I'd been broken badly
and, believe it or not,
there were no king's horses and no king's men to be
found anywhere.
I felt as if I were being stretched across The Bed of Procrustes.

The synergy of my convolutions had become convoluted,
and I couldn't think straight. It was as though my gooey fissures
had become a mass of Turkish Taffy
wrapped around my brain stem like a flagpole.
I'd become a jellied mass of expelled protoplasm
hardly able to stand on my own two feet.

At the five-star rated hospital

The much maligned and often misunderstood
Admissions Administrator
had begun to speak in benign electroconvulsives.
Her sterile language unwittingly began to shock
and squeeze out of me
what remained of my life,
as if she had become a boa constrictor.

Doctor ordered/animal tested
Punji-stick meditative shotgun prescriptions,
psychogenic cocktails camouflaged by medical science
and heaped high conglomerated mounds of research paper,
punctured my dry larynx; while shrapnel shards,
strategically placed land mines,
fueled each emotional swallow with the taste of napalm.

My kidneys and urinary tract failed me.
My crawling skin was swimming upstream
hard against the current of truth
like a determined egg-filled salmon, the blind
leading the blind into a ditch of predetermined demise.
My eyes were floating in a sea of acidic alphabet soup.
I had lost my balance, I smelled a corpse, I heard a howl.
The taste of death was stuck in my throat,
and the anxiety of bleeding ulcers,
those proliferating perforations of unleashed mustard gas
were burning my insides from the inside out.

In less than an instant, a nanosecond of physics squared,
I had become the proverbial 'dead man walking.'
I was listlessly following a plastic nurse without a face
proudly wearing a big badge on her inflated chest.
She was nonchalantly carrying her chart, a straightjacket,
and an attitude devoid of commiseration based on numbers
oozed from her molting skin.

I followed her ominous lead down the marble halls
towards the 'behavior ward' like an anxious lemming

but not before stopping at the nurses' station,
the wall of which had been plastered by arrogance.
The smell of the donuts of indifference lingered in the anesthe-
tized air;
caffeine lips and nicotine nostrils feigned compassion.

Further on down the hall we passed a bulletin board
announcing the next "Saturday Night Thorazine Shuffle Contest."
Other less obvious signs read, "Keep your hands out of the cages!"
And "Please don't feed the animals!"

Before long I knew I would see my loved one,
my dream, my queen, my everything,
locked in a nightmare of drugs and leather,
a mindless gravity-free delirious planet
of dead men walking in boots of ambiguity.

At that macabre moment of love unfeigned,
the inexplicable mathematical bond,
I felt like a muddled, mindless, meandering ox
who had been dragging a gurney behind him
through flooded, muddied, rancid rice paddies
on his way to a 'White Funeral."

Ethnic Cleansing: A War of Genes

(It's Not Just Auschwitz, Anymore)

Yesterday's ubiquitous
Rat droppings plagued and peppered Dark ages
While medieval minds elected unanimously a scapegoat.
The Chosen was some tin can chewing biblical sacrifice
Driven over the cliff by a mob
Into the pyrotechnic outstretched arms of Baal.

Today, in this age of enlightenment and understanding
Criminals are counted as victims of the superego,
And puncture wounds bleed vindication,
The bubonic vitriol of inherited predispositions
That are justified by genealogies and pigments.

All of this and more
While tempers are heated in a cauldron of hatred
And blood curdling fevers breed delirium.

In this blackboard jungle of higher learning
Psychological booby traps have been set
By pride's haughty look of a noose held high,
But it is carbuncular behavior
    Manifesting slough and suppuration.
    It is the curse of Cain born below the skin,
    Some fratricidal itch that cannot be reached
    or scratched.

Meticulous research findings, however, reveal
That an epidemiologically deeper tissue issue exists.
Under the microscope in situ
Where religious or other gangrenous nodules fidget
Minds have been filled with the pus of prejudice.

 In this geographical land of nationalistic headhunters
Darfur/Balkan/Rwandan/Syria or otherwise

Men's minds have been shrunk of love and reason.

Blood gas biases, yellow bile
And one passionate thrust of the proletariat's thighs
Are prosthetic jingoes dangling from trees.
They are leaves of laughter,
But to some they look like carrots for heroes.
To others they look like gathered scalps. Apparently,
Posthumously exhumed
                politically correct
                    crisis intervention prevailed
And eventuating discharges through obvious holes
Became perforations of the myocardium.
It has been said that life flows through here.
What then is this contamination?
This mindless intransigence,
This leukocytosis,
This mad cow disease,
This proud staphylococci,
This grass fed, cud chewing lycanthropy of Nebuchadnezzar,
                                This Dirty Dirt!
These malignant narcissistic schizophrenics
Are split heads stuffed with the poison of deceitful asps.
They are waiting like pythons to squeeze
Not hug their victims.
Some congestive lesions, swollen and anxious
Spontaneously rupture.
Others await the lance of love.

Once out in the open
The exposed necrotic tissue and pus having squirted
Demand cleansing!
Scrupulous personal hygiene is the requirement.

"What Good Shall I Do This Day?"

This quote is from Benjamin Franklin.
I recently discovered this quote.
I also discovered that he had a journal,
and that he began each day
by asking himself, in the pages of his journal,
"What good shall I do this day?"

In the evening at the conclusion of his day,
he would ask himself,
"What good have I done today?"

This quote will suit me well at the start of each day,
and will especially prepare me
to face obstacles of misunderstanding,
perhaps some form of miscommunication,
or even misrepresentation.

Besides the obvious overt acts of compassion and concern
that I have opportunities to perform,
I want to be able to do good
to those who are not good to me.

I want to be able to surprise people
by turning the other cheek.
It is easy to do good to those who do good to you,
but, "What Good Shall I Do Today,"
will be especially noteworthy in light of
abandonment, rejection, betrayal, insensitivity
and other acts that might cause me to behave badly.

I want my "What God Have I Done Today?" journal
to say, "Well done thou good and faithful servant."

Author Richard Ilnicki can be reached at:

1250 So. Pinellas Ave. #508

Tarpon Springs, Fl. 34689

crickberg1945@gmail.com

website is richardilnicki.com

His previously publications are:

Hitting Bottom

The Bibliophile

The Hatchet Man

The Birthmark and other stories

The Fossil and other stories

Godzilla Beneath The Lamp Post

Man As Horseshoe

Cover Art Design by John Winiarski